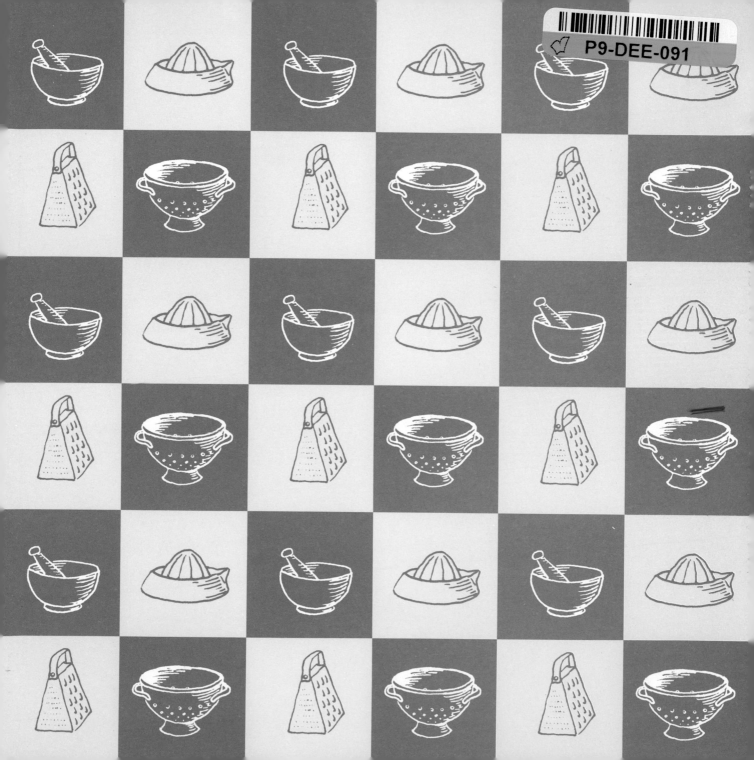

CILANTRO

CILANTRO

A Book of Recipes

INTRODUCTION BY CHRISTINE McFADDEN

LORENZ BOOKS

NEW YORK • LONDON • SYDNEY • BATH

Lorenz Books is an imprint of
Anness Publishing Limited
27 West 20th Street
New York, New York 10011

LORENZ BOOKS are available for bulk purchase for sales promotion and
for premium use. For details write or call the manager of special sales:
Lorenz Books, 27 West 20th Street, New York, New York 10011: (212) 807-6739.

Publisher: Joanna Lorenz
Senior Cookbook Editor: Linda Fraser
Project Editor: Anne Hildyard
Designer: Bill Mason
Illustrations: Anna Koska

Photographers: Karl Adamson, Edward Allwright, David Armstrong, Steve
Baxter, James Duncan, Michelle Garrett, Amanda Heywood, Patrick McLeavey
and Michael Michaels
Recipes: Alex Barker, Roz Denny, Rafi Fernandez, Shirley Gill, Deh-Ta Hsiung,
Shehzad Husain, Liz Trigg and Steven Wheeler
Food for photography: Elizabeth Wolf-Cohen, Carole Hanslip, Wendy Lee
and Annie Nichols
Stylists: Madeleine Brehaut, Hilary Guy, Clare Hunt, Maria Kelly
and Blake Minton
Jacket photography: Janine Hosegood

Printed in China

1 3 5 7 9 10 8 6 4 2

Contents

Introduction

Cilantro has always been highly esteemed in the East and in Mediterranean countries, where it has been used for thousands of years. Now, thanks to the influence of Thai and Indian restaurants and the popularity of Mexican food, westerners have taken to it with a vengeance. The smell and flavor of fresh cilantro is almost indescribable – you are either addicted to it, or would travel miles to avoid it. Cilantro can be described as pungent and exotic, almost astringent, with a touch of citrus and cumin.

In Europe, it is known as coriander. Confusingly, cilantro is also known as Chinese parsley, although it bears about as much resemblance to parsley as mint.

Cilantro is a wonderfully versatile plant. The leaves, stems, roots and seeds can all be used to create slightly different flavors.

In regions as diverse as India, China, Southeast Asia, Latin America, Portugal and the Middle East, fresh cilantro appears in all kinds of dishes either as a flavoring or garnish. It adds wonderful vibrancy and freshness to stews, curries, salads, soups, relishes, stir-fries, bean and chili dishes. In Mexican and Asian cooking, cilantro, lime and chilies

form a magical trinity that lifts seafood and salads to the realms of gastronomic euphoria.

Fresh cilantro root is one of the key ingredients in Thai food, and gives it that unmistakable, characteristic flavor. The root is pounded with garlic and black pepper to make a potent marinade for meat or fish, or it may be dried and ground and used as an ingredient in curry pastes.

The seed of the cilantro plant, called coriander, is used in Indian and Southeast Asian dishes where it adds an enticingly warm earthy flavor to curries, spice mixtures, marinades, relishes and fresh chutneys. It is also used in classic French marinated vegetable dishes.

The recipes in this book draw on exotic cuisines to enable you to experience the versatility of this plant. They begin with a mouthwatering selection of soups, appetizers and snacks, and then go on to fish and seafood dishes, in which fresh cilantro is particularly delicious. The section on meat and poultry demonstrates the different flavors of the seed and the leaf. Anyone still in doubt will be won over by the final chapter with its inspiring selection of assertively flavored vegetable and salad dishes.

Christine McFadden

TYPES OF CILANTRO

CILANTRO PLANT

The upper leaves of the plant are delicate and feathery; the lower leaves are broader and finely scalloped, similar in appearance to flat leaf parsley but with a flimsier texture. Use the lower leaves whole as a garnish, or chop a generous amount and add to dishes towards the end of cooking time for a wonderfully exotic flavor.

Chopped leaves can also be used in salads, soups, curries, sauces and dips. Fresh cilantro is also delicious in chutneys that accompany spicy dishes, and is a popular ingredient in fresh salsas.

FRESH CILANTRO ROOT

When you buy a bunch of fresh cilantro leaves, check that the roots are still attached. They not only help keep the leaves fresher but are also a useful ingredient themselves. The roots should be washed and sliced, then chopped or pounded, and added to Thai-style meat or poultry curries, stir-fries and marinades, or added to other root vegetables in stews and casseroles.

CORIANDER SEED

Like the cilantro leaf, coriander has a distinctive, pungent, spicy, flavor. The colors of the seeds range from green to cream and brown. Use them whole, or crush as desired. To bring out the warm, earthy flavor, dry-fry in a heavy pan for a few minutes before crushing.

GROUND CORIANDER

Commercially ground coriander has a fragrant aroma and a pleasant taste, mild and sweet yet slightly pungent, similar to dried orange peel.

CILANTRO PASTE

Made from fresh cilantro leaves pounded with oil, salt and acetic acid, commercially produced cilantro paste is a convenient substitute, but it lacks the vibrant flavor of the fresh leaf. It is sold in jars and can be stored in the fridge after opening for at least 12 months.

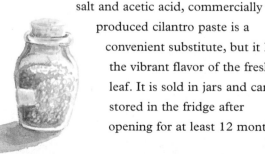

Cilantro plant

Ground coriander

Cilantro leaves

Coriander seed

Cilantro paste

Fresh cilantro root

$\mathcal{B}$ASIC $\mathcal{T}$ECHNIQUES

REMOVING STALKS

Pinch off the upper leaves from the stalks, so that a minimum amount of stalk is still attached. Then pinch off the pair of leaves that grow further down the stalk. Discard the tough stalks. Wash the leaves and dry in a salad spinner, on paper towels or in a clean dish towel.

PURÉEING CILANTRO

Remove and discard any tough stalks from 3 ounces fresh cilantro, and roughly chop the leaves. Put in a blender with 2 tablespoons each of lime juice and olive oil. Season to taste. Purée for 3 minutes, scraping the sides of the blender frequently. Add more oil or lime juice if necessary.

FREEZING CILANTRO

Finely chop a generous amount of fresh cilantro and freeze in ice cube trays. The frozen cubes can be added directly to cooked dishes. Don't use as a garnish – once defrosted, the texture deteriorates. To freeze the root, wash, wrap in foil and put in a sealed plastic bag.

BUYING FRESH CILANTRO

Choose robust, green, fresh-looking leaves. Avoid any that look limp, yellow or bruised, as they will rapidly become slimy. Avoid bunches that have a large proportion of feathery upper leaves – they are probably overgrown. Cilantro will last longer if you buy it with the roots still attached. Chinese or Thai markets are a good source.

PREPARING CORIANDER SEEDS

Coriander seeds are the principal flavoring agent in many curries. For maximum flavor, use freshly toasted and ground seeds. Frying the ground seeds in oil before adding other ingredients releases even more flavor and gives the finished dish that characteristic curry taste.

DRY-FRYING SEEDS
To enhance the flavor, dry-fry the seeds without any oil in a small, heavy pan until you smell the aroma. Stir frequently and be careful not to let them burn.

GRINDING TOASTED SEEDS
Crush coriander seeds in a mortar with a pestle, or grind them to a powder using either a spice mill or an electric coffee grinder kept especially for the purpose.

CILANTRO SALSA

Skin, seed and dice 6 medium tomatoes. Halve, seed and finely chop 1 green chili. Mix the tomatoes and chili with 2 chopped scallions, a 4-inch piece of cucumber, diced, 2 tablespoons lemon juice, ¼ cup chopped fresh cilantro and salt and ground black pepper. Transfer to a serving bowl and chill before serving.

Serves 6

Soups, Appetizers and Snacks

The lively flavor and color of fresh
cilantro adds both zest and brightness to all
kinds of first courses and snacks. It brings to life
the simplest soup or salad, and is excellent with
Asian-style appetizers.

CARROT AND CILANTRO SOUP

For maximum flavor, young carrots are best. Cilantro accentuates their sweetness in this recipe.

Serves 5–6

1 tablespoon sunflower oil

1 onion, chopped

1½ pounds carrots, chopped

2–3 fresh cilantro sprigs or
    1 teaspoon coriander

1 teaspoon grated lemon rind

2 tablespoons lemon juice

4 cups chicken stock

salt and ground black pepper

chopped fresh cilantro, to garnish

COOK'S TIP

This soup freezes well. After blending the mixture, cool it quickly, then pour it into a plastic container for freezing. Remember to allow a little room as the soup will expand as it freezes.

Heat the oil in a large saucepan. Fry the onion over gentle heat for 5 minutes, until softened but not colored. Add the chopped carrots, cilantro sprigs or coriander, lemon rind and juice. Stir well, then add the chicken stock with salt and pepper to taste.

Bring to a boil, lower the heat, cover and simmer for 15–20 minutes, occasionally checking that there is sufficient liquid. When the carrots are really tender, purée the mixture in a blender or food processor. Return to the pan, then check the seasoning.

Heat through again. Sprinkle with chopped cilantro before serving.

GAZPACHO WITH CILANTRO

Cilantro gives this Californian cold soup its distinct and original flavor.

Serves 4

1½ pounds ripe tomatoes

1 tablespoon ketchup

2 tablespoons tomato paste

¼ teaspoon sugar

½ teaspoon salt

1 teaspoon ground black pepper

¼ cup sherry or red
    wine vinegar

¾ cup olive oil

1½ cups tomato juice

1 large cucumber, about 8 ounces,
    roughly chopped

½ green bell pepper, seeded and
    roughly chopped

½ red bell pepper, seeded and
    roughly chopped

2 scallions, chopped

Tabasco sauce (optional)

¼ cup chopped fresh cilantro

croutons, to garnish

Chop 1 tomato and set it aside. Peel the remaining tomatoes, remove the seeds and chop them roughly. Transfer to a food processor or blender and pulse until just smooth, scraping the sides of the container occasionally.

Add the ketchup, tomato paste, sugar, salt, pepper, vinegar and oil and pulse 3–4 times to blend. Transfer to a large bowl. Stir in the tomato juice.

Place the cucumber and peppers in the food processor or blender and pulse until finely chopped; do not overmix.

Reserve about 2 tablespoons of the chopped vegetables for the garnish; stir the remainder into the soup. Taste for seasoning. Mix in the chopped tomato and scallions. Add a dash of Tabasco sauce if desired. Stir in half of the chopped cilantro. Chill well.

To serve, ladle into bowls and sprinkle with the reserved chopped vegetables, croutons and remaining cilantro.

CAULIFLOWER AND CILANTRO SOUP

Light and tasty, this spicy coriander-flavored soup makes a wonderfully warming first course, an appetizing quick meal or – when served chilled – a delicious summertime treat.

Serves 4–6

1 tablespoon sunflower oil

1 large potato, peeled and diced

1 small cauliflower, chopped

1 onion, chopped

1 garlic clove, crushed

1 tablespoon grated fresh ginger

2 teaspoons ground turmeric

1 teaspoon cumin seeds

1 teaspoon black mustard seeds

2 teaspoons ground coriander

4 cups vegetable stock

1¼ cups plain yogurt

salt and ground black pepper

fresh cilantro or parsley, to garnish

Heat the oil in a large saucepan, add the potato, cauliflower and onion and toss to coat. Drizzle 3 tablespoons water over the vegetables. Heat until hot and bubbling, then cover and turn the heat down. Continue cooking the mixture for about 10 minutes.

Stir in the garlic, ginger, seeds and spices. Cook for 2 more minutes, stirring occasionally. Pour in the stock and add plenty of salt and pepper. Bring to a boil, then lower the heat, cover and simmer for about 20 minutes. Stir in the yogurt, adjust the seasoning and garnish with cilantro. Serve immediately.

CHICKEN FINGERS WITH CILANTRO DIP

A refreshing cilantro yogurt makes the perfect dipping sauce for these Tandoori-style chicken fingers.

Makes about 25

¾ cup plain yogurt

1 teaspoon garam masala or
    curry powder

¼ teaspoon ground cumin

¼ teaspoon ground coriander

¼ teaspoon cayenne pepper

1 teaspoon tomato paste

1–2 garlic cloves, finely chopped

1-inch piece fresh ginger,
    peeled and finely chopped

grated rind and juice of ½ lemon

2 tablespoons chopped fresh
    cilantro or mint

1 pound boneless, skinless
    chicken breasts

For the cilantro dip

1 cup plain yogurt

2 tablespoons whipping cream

½ cucumber, peeled, seeded and
    finely chopped

2 tablespoons chopped fresh
    cilantro or mint

salt and ground black pepper

Prepare the cilantro dip first. Combine all the ingredients in a bowl and season with salt and ground black pepper. Cover and chill until ready to serve.

Put the yogurt, spices, tomato paste, garlic, ginger, lemon rind and juice and herbs in a food processor or blender, and process until smooth. Pour into a shallow dish.

Freeze the chicken breasts for 5 minutes to firm them slightly, then slice them in half horizontally. Cut the slices into ¾-inch strips and add to the marinade. Toss to coat well. Cover and chill for 6–8 hours or overnight.

Preheat the broiler and line a baking sheet with foil. Using a slotted spoon, remove the chicken from the marinade and arrange the pieces in a single layer on the baking sheet. Scrunch up the chicken slightly so it makes wavy shapes. Broil for 4–5 minutes until brown and just cooked, turning once. Thread 1–2 pieces onto toothpicks or short skewers and serve with the cilantro dip.

GRILLED GREEN MUSSELS WITH CILANTRO

Large green shelled mussels have a more distinctive flavor than the small black variety, and they are particularly delicious with this cilantro crumb topping.

Serves 4

3 tablespoons chopped fresh cilantro

3 tablespoons chopped fresh parsley

1 garlic clove, crushed

pinch of ground coriander

2 tablespoons butter, softened

½ cup whole wheat
    bread crumbs

ground black pepper

12 green mussels or 24 small mussels
    on the half-shell

chopped fresh cilantro or parsley,
    to garnish

COOK'S TIP

Use a mezzaluna (a twin-handled curved blade) to chop the herbs, or put them in a large mug and snip them with kitchen scissors.

Chop the cilantro and parsley finely. Beat the garlic, herbs, ground coriander and butter in a bowl with a wooden spoon, then stir in the bread crumbs and ground black pepper. Preheat the broiler.

Spoon a little of the mixture onto each mussel. Arrange the mussels in a broiler pan, using crumpled foil to keep them upright, if necessary. Broil for 2 minutes. Serve garnished with chopped cilantro.

HOT CILANTRO SHRIMP

Don't stint on the cilantro when making this hot and spicy appetizer. Added at the last minute, it retains its flavor and color better.

Serves 4–6

1 garlic clove, crushed

$\frac{1}{2}$-inch piece fresh ginger, peeled and chopped

1 small fresh red chili, seeded and chopped

2 teaspoons sugar

1 tablespoon light soy sauce

1 tablespoon vegetable oil

1 teaspoon sesame oil

juice of 1 lime

salt, to taste

1$\frac{1}{2}$ pounds whole raw shrimp

1 cup cherry tomatoes

$\frac{1}{2}$ cucumber, cut into chunks

1 small bunch cilantro, roughly chopped

Combine the garlic, ginger, chili and sugar in a mortar and pound to a paste with a pestle. Add the soy sauce, vegetable and sesame oils, lime juice and salt. Arrange the shrimp in a single layer in a shallow dish, pour the marinade over them and coat well. Cover and marinate for as long as possible, preferably for 8 hours.

Preheat the broiler. Drain the shrimp and thread them onto bamboo skewers, alternating with the tomatoes and cucumber. Grill for 3–4 minutes, brushing occasionally with any remaining marinade. Transfer to a platter, sprinkle with the cilantro and serve.

AVOCADO, CILANTRO AND FISH SALAD

Avocado and smoked fish make a good combination, especially when flavored with cilantro and spices.

Serves 4

1 tablespoon butter or margarine

½ onion, finely sliced

1 teaspoon mustard seeds

8 ounces smoked mackerel, skinned
   and flaked

2 tablespoons chopped fresh cilantro

2 firm tomatoes, peeled and chopped

1 tablespoon lemon juice

For the salad

2 avocados

½ cucumber

1 tablespoon lemon juice

2 firm tomatoes

1 green chili

salt and ground black pepper

VARIATION

*Smoked haddock or cod are
good in this salad, or use
mackerel and haddock.*

Melt the butter in a frying pan, add the onion and mustard seeds and fry for about 5 minutes, until the onion is soft. Add the fish, chopped cilantro, tomatoes and lemon juice and cook over low heat for 2–3 minutes. Remove from the heat and cool.

Make the salad. Cut the avocados in half and remove the pits and peel. Slice the avocados and cucumber thinly. Place together in a bowl and sprinkle with the lemon juice. Slice the tomatoes. Chop the chili finely, discarding the seeds.

Spoon the fish mixture onto the center of a serving plate. Arrange the avocados, cucumber and tomatoes decoratively around the outside of the fish. Alternatively, spoon a quarter of the fish mixture onto each of four serving plates and divide the avocados, cucumber and tomatoes equally among them. Sprinkle with the chopped chili and a little salt and pepper and serve.

CHERRY TOMATOES WITH GUACAMOLE AND CILANTRO

Cherry tomatoes stuffed with a creamy cilantro-flavored guacamole make perfect nibbles.

Makes 24

24 cherry tomatoes

1 large ripe avocado

¼ cup cream cheese

3–4 dashes of Tabasco sauce, or to taste

grated rind and juice of ½ lime

2 tablespoons chopped fresh cilantro

salt

COOK'S TIP

The tomatoes can be prepared a day in advance. Store in the fridge, ready for filling, upside down in a covered container. Don't be tempted to make the guacamole ahead of time, though, as it may discolor.

Cut a slice from the bottom of each tomato, then use the handle of a small spoon to scoop out the seeds. Sprinkle the cavities with salt. Drain the tomatoes upside down on paper towels for at least 30 minutes.

Cut the avocado in half and discard the pit. Scoop the flesh into a food processor or blender and add the cream cheese. Process until very smooth, scraping down the sides of the bowl once or twice. Season with salt and Tabasco sauce, then add the lime rind and juice. Toss in half of the chopped cilantro and process to blend.

Spoon the mixture into a piping bag fitted with a medium star nozzle. Pipe swirls into the tomatoes. Arrange on a platter, sprinkle with the remaining cilantro and serve.

FALAFEL

A typical snack food in Israel, crispy falafel seasoned with fresh cilantro are served in warm pita bread.

Serves 4

1¼ cups dried chick-peas

3 garlic cloves, crushed

1 teaspoon cumin seeds

1 teaspoon coriander seeds

1 handful fresh cilantro,
  finely chopped

1 handful flat leaf parsley,
  finely chopped

1 teaspoon salt

¼ teaspoon chili powder

1 tablespoon lemon juice

1 teaspoon baking powder

oil, for deep frying

ground black pepper

pita bread and hummus, to serve

Soak the chick-peas overnight in water to cover. Drain thoroughly and transfer to a saucepan. Add fresh water to cover and bring to a boil. Cook until the chick-peas are soft – this can take from 1½ to 4 hours. Drain the chick-peas and put them in a food processor or blender.

Using a pestle, grind the garlic with the cumin and coriander seeds in a mortar. Process the chick-peas until they are broken up. Add the garlic paste, fresh herbs, salt and chili powder. Process until smooth.

Add the lemon juice, taste for seasoning and add ground pepper or more spice to taste. Scrape into a bowl and let stand for about 30 minutes.

Stir in the baking powder and form the mixture into small balls. Fry in hot oil for 2–3 minutes or until the falafel are golden. Drain and serve with pita bread and hummus.

Fish and Seafood

With its intensely exotic aroma, cilantro is
delicious with fish and seafood, particularly
when combined with the clean, bright, astringent
flavors of other aromatics such as limes, chilies,
ginger and lemongrass.

BAKED TUNA WITH CILANTRO CRUST

There's nothing like a fresh cilantro marinade to liven up the flavor of fresh meaty tuna steaks.

Serves 4

finely grated rind of 1 lemon

1 teaspoon black peppercorns

½ small onion, finely chopped

2 tablespoons chopped fresh cilantro

4 fresh tuna steaks,
  about 6 ounces each

½ cup olive oil

For the salsa

1 mango, peeled and diced

finely grated rind and juice of 1 lime

½ fresh red chili, seeded and
  finely chopped

COOK'S TIP

Tuna is an excellent choice for the barbecue. Cook the steaks on the grill over moderately hot coals.

Make the salsa. Mix the mango, lime rind and juice and chili in a bowl and let marinate for at least 1 hour.

Grind the lemon rind, black peppercorns, onion and cilantro to a coarse paste, using a mortar and pestle or a coffee grinder. Spoon a quarter of the mixture onto one side of each tuna steak, pressing on well.

Heat the olive oil in a heavy frying pan until it begins to smoke. Add the tuna, paste-side down, and fry until a crust forms. Lower the heat and turn the steaks to cook for 1 more minute. Pat off any excess oil with paper towels and serve with the salsa.

THAI FISH SALAD WITH CILANTRO

Treat yourself to this fish salad with its tantalizing mixture of cilantro, coconut and chili flavours.

Serves 4

fillet of red mullet, about 12 ounces

1 bag mixed salad leaves

½ cucumber

1 papaya, peeled and sliced

1 mango, peeled and sliced

1 large ripe tomato, cut into wedges

3 scallions, sliced

For the marinade

1 teaspoon coriander seeds

1 teaspoon fennel seeds

½ teaspoon cumin seeds

1 teaspoon superfine sugar

½ teaspoon hot chili sauce

2 tablespoons garlic oil

salt

For the dressing

1 tablespoon creamed coconut

¼ cup peanut oil

finely grated rind and juice of 1 lime

1 red chili, seeded and chopped

1 teaspoon granulated sugar

3 tablespoons chopped fresh cilantro

Cut the fish into even strips and place in a single layer in a shallow dish. Make the marinade. Put the coriander, fennel and cumin seeds in a mortar. Add the sugar and crush well. Stir in the chili sauce, garlic oil and salt. Spread the marinade over the fish, cover and let stand in a cool place for at least 20 minutes – longer if you have time.

Make the dressing. Place the creamed coconut in a screw-top jar with 3 tablespoons boiling water and a pinch of salt. Stir until dissolved. Add the oil, lime rind and juice, chili, sugar and chopped fresh cilantro. Close the jar tightly, shake well to mix and set aside.

Wash and spin the salad leaves. Peel and cut the cucumber into batons. Place them in a bowl and add the papaya, mango, tomato and scallions. Pour on the dressing, toss well, then distribute among four large plates.

Heat a large non-stick frying pan, add the fish and cook for 5 minutes, turning once. Arrange the cooked fish on the salad and serve.

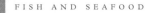
CORIANDER-MARINATED FISH STEAKS

Ground coriander and fresh cilantro combine to make a marinade and a sauce for succulent fish steaks.

Serves 4

4 halibut or cod steaks or cutlets,
  about 6 ounces each
juice of 1 lemon
1 garlic clove, crushed
1 teaspoon paprika
1 teaspoon ground coriander
½ teaspoon dried tarragon
plain flour, for dusting
¼ cup olive oil, plus extra for frying
  onion
1¼ cups fish stock
2 red chilies, seeded and
  finely chopped
2 tablespoons chopped fresh cilantro
1 red onion, sliced into rings
salt and ground black pepper

Place the fish in a single layer in a shallow dish. Mix the lemon juice, garlic, paprika, ground coriander, tarragon and a little salt and pepper in a bowl. Spoon the mixture over the fish, cover loosely with plastic wrap and marinate for a few hours, or overnight, in the fridge.

Dust the fish with flour. Gently heat the oil in a large non-stick frying pan. Fry the fish for a few minutes on each side, until golden brown all over, then pour the fish stock into the pan. Cover and simmer for about 5 minutes, until the fish is thoroughly cooked.

Add the chilies and half the chopped cilantro to the pan. Simmer for 5 more minutes, then transfer the fish and sauce to a serving plate. Keep it hot.

Wipe the pan, heat some oil and stir-fry the onion until speckled brown. Scatter the remaining chopped cilantro over the fish, and serve.

SALMON WITH SIZZLING CILANTRO

This superb salmon dish combines fresh fish with the distinctive tang of cilantro.

Serves 4

4 salmon steaks, about 6 ounces each

¼ cup chopped fresh cilantro

3 tablespoons grated fresh ginger

3 scallions, finely chopped

¼ cup soy sauce, plus extra
   to serve

5 tablespoons olive oil

salt and ground black pepper

lettuce and cilantro sprigs,
   to garnish

Season the salmon steaks on both sides with salt and pepper. Prepare a steamer (see Cook's Tip), add the salmon steaks, cover and steam for 7–8 minutes, until the fish is opaque throughout.

Place the steamed salmon steaks on warmed plates. Divide the chopped cilantro between them, mounding it on top of the fish. Sprinkle with the ginger and then the scallions. Drizzle 1 tablespoon of soy sauce over each salmon steak. Heat the oil in a small heavy saucepan until very hot. Spoon the hot oil over each salmon steak and serve immediately, with more soy sauce, if desired. Garnish with lettuce and cilantro sprigs.

COOK'S TIP

If you do not own a steamer, cook the fish steaks on a lightly buttered plate over a pan of simmering water. Cover the fish with waxed paper or invert a second plate on top.

FISH KEBABS WITH CILANTRO

Skewers of fresh fish and vegetables basted in a cilantro marinade make irresistible kebabs.

Serves 4

10 ounces cod fillets, or any other
  firm white fish fillets, skinned
3 tablespoons lemon juice
1 teaspoon grated fresh ginger
2 fresh green chilies, finely chopped
1 tablespoon finely chopped
  fresh cilantro
1 tablespoon finely chopped
  fresh mint
1 teaspoon ground coriander
1 teaspoon salt
1 red bell pepper
1 green bell pepper
½ cauliflower
8–10 button mushrooms
8 cherry tomatoes
1 tablespoon soy oil
saffron rice, to serve

Cut the fish fillets into large chunks. Mix the lemon juice, ginger, chilies, fresh cilantro, mint, ground coriander and salt in a mixing bowl. Add the fish chunks, mix to coat and marinate for about 30 minutes.

Cut the red and green bell peppers into large squares, discarding the core and seeds from each. Divide the cauliflower into individual florets. Preheat the broiler.

Thread the peppers, cauliflower florets, mushrooms and cherry tomatoes alternately with the fish pieces on to four skewers. Brush the kebabs with the oil and any remaining marinade. Transfer to a flameproof dish and grill for 7–10 minutes or until the fish is opaque throughout. Serve on a bed of saffron rice.

RED SNAPPER WITH CILANTRO

Mexico is the source of this exciting fish dish. The cilantro cooks down with the chilies, onion and pan juices to make a delicious sauce.

Serves 4

2 pounds red snapper fillets, or other
   white fish fillets
6 tablespoons lime or lemon juice
¼ cup olive oil
1 onion, finely chopped
2 cups fresh cilantro,
   finely chopped
2 drained canned jalapeño chilies,
   rinsed, seeded and sliced
salt and ground black pepper
cilantro sprigs, to garnish
rice with tomatoes, to serve

P lace the fish in a shallow dish. Season with salt and pepper and drizzle the lime or lemon juice over it. Cover and set aside for 15 minutes.

Preheat the oven to 350°F. Heat all but 1 tablespoon of the oil in a frying pan and sauté the onion until soft. Meanwhile, using the reserved oil, thinly coat the bottom of an ovenproof dish that is just large enough to hold the fish fillets in a single layer. Arrange the fish in the dish and pour on any remaining marinating liquid. Top with the sautéed onion and the oil from the pan.

Sprinkle on the cilantro and chilies. Bake for 20–25 minutes or until the fish is opaque throughout. Garnish with cilantro sprigs and serve with rice.

SHRIMP AND CILANTRO SALAD

Shrimp and cilantro help to provide a wonderful balance of colors, textures and flavors in this salad.

Serves 4

1 ripe tomato, peeled

½ iceberg lettuce, shredded

1 small onion, shredded

1 small bunch fresh
   cilantro, shredded

1 tablespoon lemon juice

1 pound cooked shrimp, peeled
   and deveined

1 Granny Smith apple

salt

For the dressing

5 tablespoons mayonnaise

1 tablespoon mild curry paste

1 tablespoon ketchup

To decorate

8 whole shrimp

8 lemon wedges

4 fresh cilantro sprigs

Cut the peeled tomato in half, squeeze out all the seeds, then cut the flesh into large dice.

Mix the lettuce, onion and cilantro with the tomato, moisten with lemon juice and season with salt.

Make the dressing. Combine the mayonnaise, curry paste and ketchup in a small bowl. Stir in enough water (2 tablespoons) to thin the dressing, and season to taste with salt.

Add the cooked shrimp to the dressing. Peel the apple and grate it into the mixture. Divide the shredded lettuce mixture between four plates or bowls. Pile the shrimp dressing in the center of each and decorate with two whole shrimp, two lemon wedges and a cilantro sprig.

CILANTRO-COATED SHRIMP

Taste sensations come immediately when you bite into one of these shrimp. First, there is golden grilled cheese, then a crisp cilantro crust and finally succulent shellfish.

Serves 4

¾ cup cornstarch

1–2 teaspoons cayenne pepper

2½ teaspoons ground cumin

1 teaspoon salt

2 tablespoons chopped fresh cilantro

flour, for dredging

2 pounds large raw shrimp, peeled
    and deveined

¼ cup vegetable oil

1 cup grated aged Cheddar cheese

lime wedges and tomato salsa,
    to serve

COOK'S TIP

When preparing the shrimp, remove the heads, but leave the tails intact.

Mix the cornstarch, cayenne pepper, cumin, salt and cilantro in a bowl. Have two shallow bowls ready, one holding water and the other the flour for dredging.

Coat the shrimp lightly in flour, then dip in water and roll in the cornstarch mixture to coat.

Heat the oil in a non-stick frying pan. When hot, add the shrimp, in batches if necessary. Cook for 2–3 minutes on each side, until they are opaque. Drain on paper towels.

Place the shrimp in a single layer in a large baking dish, or individual dishes. Sprinkle the cheese evenly over the top. Grill for 2–3 minutes, until the cheese melts. Serve immediately, with lime wedges and tomato salsa.

CILANTRO CRAB WITH COCONUT

Coriander seeds add a pungent taste to this spicy dish – simply serve it with plain warm nan.

Serves 4

½ cup dried unsweetened coconut
    flakes

2 garlic cloves, roughly chopped

2-inch piece fresh ginger,
    peeled and grated

½ teaspoon cumin seeds

1 small cinnamon stick, broken

½ teaspoon ground turmeric

2 dried red chilies, crumbled

1 tablespoon coriander seeds

½ teaspoon poppy seeds

1 tablespoon vegetable oil

1 onion, sliced

1 small green bell pepper, cut into strips

16 crab claws

fresh cilantro sprigs, crushed,
    to garnish

⅔ cup plain yogurt, to serve

P lace the dried coconut, garlic, ginger, cumin seeds, cinnamon, turmeric, chilies, and coriander and poppy seeds in a food processor or blender. Process until well blended.

Heat the oil in a wok and fry the onion until soft, but not colored. Stir in the green bell pepper and stir-fry for 1 minute, then remove the vegetables with a slotted spoon. Set aside.

Heat the wok again. Add the crab claws, stir-fry for 2 minutes, then briefly return all the spiced vegetables to the wok. Toss over the heat for about 1 minute. Garnish with fresh cilantro sprigs and serve with the cooling plain yogurt.

Meat and Poultry

Cilantro leaf and coriander seeds heighten the flavor of all types of meat and poultry dishes, from slow-cooked casseroles to speedy stir-fries. The fragrant spiciness helps to temper any richness and is especially good with lamb and chicken.

BEEF AND CILANTRO RAGOUT

Based on the ever-popular couscous recipes of North Africa, this cilantro-spiced ragoût mixes ground beef with a mixture of fresh vegetables.

Serves 4

1 tablespoon oil
4 cups ground beef
1 garlic clove, crushed
1 onion, quartered
2 tablespoons flour
²⁄₃ cup dry white wine
²⁄₃ cup beef stock
2 baby turnips, chopped
4 ounces rutabaga, chopped
2 carrots, cut into chunks
2 zucchini, cut into chunks
1 tablespoon chopped fresh cilantro
1 teaspoon ground coriander
1½ cups couscous
salt and ground black pepper
fresh cilantro, to garnish

Heat the oil in a large saucepan. Add the ground beef and fry for 5 minutes, stirring frequently. Add the garlic and onion. Cook for 3 more minutes, then stir in the flour. Cook for 1 minute. Add the wine and stock and bring to a boil, stirring constantly.

Add the prepared vegetables with the fresh cilantro and ground coriander. Stir in salt and pepper to taste. Lower the heat, cover and cook for 15 minutes.

Meanwhile, place the couscous in a bowl. Pour in boiling water to cover. Let stand for 10 minutes. Drain and place the couscous in a lined steamer or colander. Remove the lid from the saucepan containing the vegetables and place the steamer on top. Steam the couscous over the pan for 30 more minutes. Garnish with fresh cilantro and serve.

SPICY MEATBALLS WITH CORIANDER

Coriander is the traditional flavoring for these tasty Indonesian meatballs.

Makes 24

1 large onion, roughly chopped

*1–2 fresh red chilies, seeded
    and chopped*

2 garlic cloves, crushed

½-inch cube terasi, prepared

1 tablespoon coriander seeds

1 teaspoon cumin seeds

4 cups lean ground beef

2 teaspoons dark soy sauce

1 teaspoon dark brown sugar

juice of ½ lemon

a little beaten egg

oil, for shallow frying

salt and ground black pepper

fresh cilantro sprigs, to garnish

COOK'S TIP
*Terasi is a pungent shrimp
paste, also known as blachan,
kapi or ngapi. It should be
heated gently before use.*

Put the onion, chilies, garlic and terasi in a food processor or blender. Process in bursts; do not overmix or the onion will become too wet and spoil the consistency of the meatballs. Dry-fry the coriander and cumin seeds in a preheated frying pan for about 1 minute, to release the aroma. Do not brown. Transfer to a mortar and grind with a pestle.

Put the ground beef in a large mixing bowl. Stir in the onion mixture. Add the ground coriander and cumin, soy sauce, sugar and lemon juice. Stir in salt and pepper to taste, bind with a little beaten egg and shape into small, uniform balls.

Chill the meatballs briefly to firm them up, if necessary. Fry them in shallow oil, turning often, until cooked through and browned. This will take 4–5 minutes, depending on their size.

Remove from the pan with a slotted spoon, drain well on paper towels and serve, garnished with cilantro sprigs.

CHICKEN AND CILANTRO PIZZA

Cilantro and chili are used to flavor mushrooms and chicken for an unusual pizza.

Serves 3–4

3 tablespoons olive oil

*12 ounces boneless, skinless chicken
    breasts, cut into thin strips*

1 bunch scallions, sliced

1 fresh red chili, seeded and chopped

*1 red bell pepper, seeded and cut into
    thin strips*

*3 ounces fresh shiitake mushrooms,
    wiped and sliced*

1 pizza crust, 10–12 inches in diameter

1 tablespoon chili oil

¼ cup chopped fresh cilantro

5 ounces mozzarella cheese

salt and ground black pepper

Preheat the oven to 425°F. Heat 2 tablespoons of the olive oil in a wok or large frying pan. Add the chicken, scallions, chili, pepper and mushrooms and stir-fry over high heat for 2–3 minutes, until the chicken is firm but still slightly pink inside. Sprinkle on salt and pepper to taste, pour off any excess oil, then set the chicken mixture aside to cool.

Brush the pizza crust base with chili oil. Stir the cilantro into the chicken mixture, spoon it over the pizza and drizzle on the remaining olive oil.

Grate the mozzarella cheese and sprinkle it over the pizza. Bake for 15–20 minutes, until the crust is crisp and golden. Serve immediately.

COOK'S TIP

*Use the spicy chicken mixture
as a filling for baked potatoes
or pita pockets. Or simply pile
it on toasted ciabatta bread.*

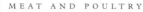

SPICY CILANTRO CHICKEN

Chicken thighs basted in a spicy cilantro marinade are perfect for parties or lively midweek meals.

Serves 6

12 chicken thighs

6 tablespoons lemon juice

1 teaspoon grated fresh ginger

2 garlic cloves, crushed

2 dried red chilies, crumbled

1 teaspoon salt

1 teaspoon light brown sugar

2 tablespoons clear honey

2 tablespoons chopped fresh cilantro

1 fresh green chili, finely chopped

2 tablespoons vegetable oil

fresh cilantro sprigs, to garnish

COOK'S TIP

Adjust the quantity of dried chilies to suit the diners. Remove the seeds if a milder flavor is preferred.

Prick the chicken thighs with a fork, rinse, pat dry and set aside in a bowl. Mix the lemon juice, ginger, garlic, crumbled dried red chilies, salt, sugar and honey in a large mixing bowl. Add the chicken thighs and coat well. Cover and set aside for about 45 minutes.

Preheat the broiler. Add the fresh cilantro and chopped green chili to the chicken thigh mixture, then arrange the thighs in a flameproof dish. Pour on any remaining marinade, then baste with the oil, using a pastry brush.

Broil the chicken thighs for 15–20 minutes, turning and basting occasionally, until cooked through and browned. Transfer to a serving dish, garnish with the fresh cilantro sprigs and serve.

STIR-FRIED CILANTRO CHICKEN

This satisfying stir-fry, flavored with cilantro and fresh coriander, is perfect for a speedy supper or lunch.

Serves 4

10 ounces Chinese egg noodles

2 tablespoons vegetable oil

3 scallions, chopped

1 garlic clove, crushed

1-inch piece of fresh
*   ginger, grated*

1 teaspoon hot paprika

1 teaspoon ground coriander

3 skinless, boneless chicken
*   breasts, sliced*

1 cup sugar-snap peas, trimmed

4 ounces baby corn, halved

1 cup fresh beansprouts

1 tablespoon cornstarch

3 tablespoons soy sauce

3 tablespoons lemon juice

1 tablespoon granulated sugar

3 tablespoons chopped fresh cilantro,
*   to garnish*

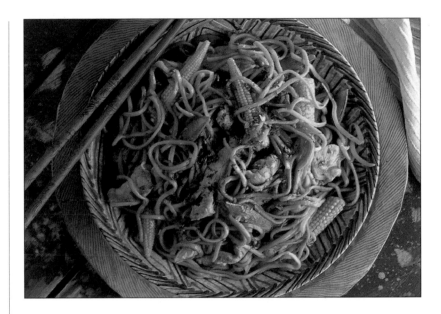

Bring a large saucepan of salted water to a boil. Add the noodles and cook according to the package instructions. Drain, cover and keep warm.

Heat the oil in a wok or large heavy frying pan. Add the scallions and cook over low heat. Mix in the garlic, ginger, paprika, ground coriander and chicken, then stir-fry for 3–4 minutes. Add the sugar-snap peas, corn and beansprouts and steam briefly. Add the noodles and toss over the heat.

Combine the cornstarch, soy sauce, lemon juice and sugar in a small bowl. Add to the wok and simmer briefly to thicken. Serve garnished with chopped cilantro.

LAMB AND CILANTRO FILO PIE

Crisp golden filo contrasts with a moist lamb filling that is lightly spiced with coriander and cumin.

Serves 4

1 tablespoon oil

4 cups ground lamb

1 red onion, sliced

2 tablespoons chopped fresh cilantro

2 tablespoons flour

1¼ cups lamb stock

½ cup drained canned chick-peas

1 teaspoon ground cumin

½ pound filo pastry

2 tablespoons butter, melted

½ cup dried apricots

1 zucchini, sliced

salt and ground black pepper

freshly cooked vegetables, to serve

Preheat the oven to 375°F Heat the oil in a large pan. Add the ground lamb and cook for 5 minutes. Stir in the onion, fresh cilantro and flour and cook for 1 more minute.

Pour in the stock and chick-peas. Add salt and pepper to taste and stir in the cumin. Cook for 20 minutes, stirring occasionally.

Line a deep ovenproof dish with four sheets of filo pastry, brushing each sheet lightly with melted butter as it is placed in the dish. Spoon in the lamb mixture. Top with dried apricots and zucchini slices.

Lay two sheets of filo pastry on top of the filling and brush with melted butter. Fold or scrunch the remaining sheets on top. Pour on the rest of the butter and bake for 40 minutes. Serve immediately with a selection of freshly cooked vegetables.

COOK'S TIP

Cover any filo sheets not being used with plastic wrap as the pastry dries out very rapidly.

Vegetable Dishes and Salads

Cilantro is a superb addition to gutsy vegetable dishes and salads. The assertive flavor of the leaf adds sparkle and zest to green leafy vegetables, while the spicy seed adds fragrance to pilafs and eggplant dishes.

CARROT AND CILANTRO SOUFFLES

Depending on how it is used, cilantro can give a robust or a delicate flavor. Here, it perfectly complements carrots in these light-as-air soufflés.

Serves 4

1 pound young carrots

2 tablespoons chopped fresh cilantro

4 eggs, separated

salt and ground black pepper

Peel the carrots, but do not slice them. Bring a saucepan of lightly salted water to a boil. Add the carrots and cook for 20 minutes or until tender. Drain, and process until smooth in a food processor or blender.

Preheat the oven to 400°F. Grease four individual ramekins. Season the puréed carrots well, and stir in the chopped cilantro. Fold in the egg yolks.

In a separate bowl, whisk the egg whites until stiff. Fold the egg whites into the carrot mixture and pour into the prepared ramekins. Bake for about 20 minutes or until the soufflés are risen and golden. Serve immediately.

BEAN AND CILANTRO SALAD

A cilantro dressing poured over beans makes a healthy and extremely tasty salad.

Serves 4

1½ cups dried pinto beans, soaked
   and drained
1 bay leaf
3 tablespoons coarse salt
2 ripe tomatoes, diced
4 scallions, finely chopped

For the dressing

¼ cup fresh lemon juice
6 tablespoons olive oil
1 garlic clove, crushed
3 tablespoons chopped fresh cilantro
salt and ground black pepper
cilantro sprig, to garnish

VARIATION
For a quick and easy salad, use a drained can (15 ounces) of chick-peas or butter beans. Just simmer for a few minutes with the bay leaf before using.

Put the pinto beans in a large saucepan. Add fresh cold water to cover and the bay leaf. Bring to a boil, then lower the heat, cover and simmer for 30 minutes. Add the salt and simmer for 30 minutes or until the beans are tender. Drain, discarding the bay leaf. Set aside to cool slightly.

Make the dressing. In a bowl, mix the lemon juice and 1 teaspoon salt until dissolved. Gradually whisk in the oil until the dressing is thick. Add the garlic and cilantro, with pepper to taste.

While the beans are still warm, place them in a large bowl. Add the dressing and toss to coat. Let the beans cool completely.

Add the tomatoes and scallions and toss to coat evenly. Allow the salad to stand for at least 30 minutes before serving, garnished with a cilantro sprig.

NUT AND CILANTRO PILAF

Ground coriander adds fragrance to basmati rice in this perfect pilaf.

Serves 4–6

1 cup basmati rice

1–2 tablespoons sunflower oil

1 onion, chopped

1 garlic clove, crushed

1 large carrot, coarsely grated

1 teaspoon cumin seeds

2 teaspoons black mustard
   seeds (optional)

2 teaspoons ground coriander

4 cardamom pods

2 cups vegetable
   stock or water

1 bay leaf

¾ cup unsalted nuts

salt and ground black pepper

fresh chopped cilantro, to garnish

Put the rice in a large bowl of cold water. Swill the grains around with your hands, then pour out the cloudy water. Repeat this action about five times. If there is time, soak the rice for 30 minutes, then drain well in a sieve.

Heat the oil in a large shallow pan. Fry the onion, garlic and carrot over low heat for a few minutes, then stir in the rice, seeds and spices. Cook for 1–2 minutes, stirring, so that the grains are all coated in the oil.

Pour in the stock, add the bay leaf and season well. Bring to a boil, lower the heat, cover and simmer gently for 10 minutes. Without lifting the lid, remove the pan from the heat and let sit for 5 minutes; this helps the rice firm up and finish cooking. When the rice is fully cooked, there will be small steam holes in the center. Discard the bay leaf and cardamom pods.

Stir in the nuts and check the seasoning. Sprinkle the chopped cilantro over the pilaf and serve immediately

FRAGRANT CILANTRO RICE

A soft, fluffy rice dish, perfumed with fresh lemongrass and flavored with cilantro.

Serves 4

1 cup brown basmati rice

1 tablespoon olive oil

1 onion, chopped

1-inch piece fresh ginger, peeled and
  finely chopped

1½ teaspoons coriander seeds

1½ teaspoons cumin seeds

1 piece lemongrass, finely chopped

grated rind of 2 limes

3 cups vegetable stock

4 tablespoons chopped fresh cilantro

lime wedges, to serve

COOK'S TIP

*Other varieties of rice, such as
white basmati or long grain,
can be used for this dish, but
you will need to adjust the
cooking times accordingly.*

Put the rice into a large bowl of cold water. Swill the grains around with your hands, then pour out the cloudy water (the rice will quickly sink to the bottom). Repeat this action about five times. If there is time, soak the rice for about 5 minutes.

Heat the oil in a large saucepan and add the onion, spices, lemongrass and grated lime rind. Cook gently for 2–3 minutes.

Add the rice, turning it in the mixture to coat the grains. Cook for 1 more minute, then add the stock and bring to a boil. Reduce the heat to very low and cover the pan. Cook gently for 30 minutes, then check the rice; if it is still crunchy, cover the pan again and let sit for 3–5 more minutes. Remove from the heat.

Stir in the fresh cilantro, fluff up the grains, cover the pan and let sit for 10 minutes. Serve immediately, with lime wedges.

CILANTRO AND VEGETABLE STEW

Cilantro is used in combination with chick-peas and eggplant in this spicy West African stew.

Serves 3–4

3 tablespoons olive oil

1 red onion, chopped

3 garlic cloves, crushed

*¼ pound sweet potatoes, peeled
  and diced*

1 large eggplant, diced

15 ounce-can chick-peas, drained

1 teaspoon dried tarragon

½ teaspoon dried thyme

1 teaspoon ground cumin

1 teaspoon ground turmeric

½ teaspoon ground allspice

*5 drained canned plum tomatoes,
  chopped, plus ¼ cup of the can
  juices*

6 dried apricots

2½ cups vegetable stock

*1 fresh green chili, seeded and
  finely chopped*

2 tablespoons chopped fresh cilantro

salt and ground black pepper

Heat the olive oil in a large saucepan over medium heat. Add the onion, garlic and sweet potatoes and cook for about 5 minutes, until the onion has softened slightly.

Stir in the diced eggplant, then add the chick-peas, herbs and spices. Stir well to mix and cook over low heat for a few minutes.

Add the tomatoes and the reserved juice from the can, with the apricots, stock and chili. Stir in salt and pepper to taste. Bring slowly to a boil and cook for about 15 minutes or until the sweet potatoes are tender. Add the fresh cilantro, stir and adjust the seasoning if necessary. Serve immediately.

PLANTAIN AND BANANA SALAD WITH CILANTRO SAUCE

The plantains and bananas are cooked in their skins to retain their soft texture. This helps them to absorb the full flavor of the cilantro dressing.

Serves 4

2 firm yellow plantains

3 green bananas

1 garlic clove, crushed

1 red onion, halved and thinly sliced

2 tablespoons chopped fresh cilantro

3 tablespoons sunflower oil

4 teaspoons malt vinegar

salt and ground black pepper

Slit the plantains and bananas lengthwise along their natural ridges, then cut them in half and place in a large saucepan. Pour water over them to cover, add a little salt and bring to a boil. Boil gently for 20 minutes until tender, then remove the bananas and plantains from the water. When they are cool enough to handle, peel and slice.

Put the plantain and banana slices into a bowl and add the garlic and onion. Mix well.

Add the cilantro, oil and vinegar, with salt and pepper to taste. Toss together to mix, then serve as an accompaniment to a main dish, such as Spicy Cilantro Chicken.

WARM CHICKEN SALAD WITH SESAME AND CILANTRO DRESSING

Serving this salad warm makes the most of the wonderful sesame and cilantro flavorings.

Serves 6

4 skinless, boneless chicken breasts

2 cups snow peas

2 heads decorative lettuce, such as
lollo rosso or feuille de chêne,
torn into pieces

3 carrots, peeled and cut into
small matchsticks

2¼ cups button mushrooms, sliced

5 strips bacon

1 tablespoon chopped fresh cilantro,
to garnish

salt

For the dressing

½ cup lemon juice

2 tablespoons whole-grain mustard

1 cup olive oil

5 tablespoons sesame oil

1 teaspoon coriander seeds, crushed

Mix the dressing ingredients. Place the chicken breasts in a dish and pour on half of the dressing. Cover and marinate overnight in the fridge.

Bring a pan of lightly salted water to a boil. Add the snow peas and cook for 2 minutes. Drain, refresh under cold water and drain again.

Mix the lettuce, snow peas, carrots and mushrooms in a bowl. Toss to mix, then divide among six individual dishes. Preheat the oven to 375°F.

Arrange the chicken breasts on a pan and cook for 8–10 minutes until cooked through. Meanwhile, heat the bacon in a dry frying pan until the fat runs, then fry until crisp.

Slice the chicken thinly and arrange on the salads. Crumble the bacon on top. Add the reserved dressing to the fat in the pan and heat briefly. Pour a little dressing over each salad, garnish with fresh cilantro and serve.

BEANSPROUTS WITH CILANTRO

This simple, delicious dish is given extra zest by the addition of fresh cilantro. For the freshest results, sprout your own beans.

Serves 3–4

*2 tablespoons sunflower or
    peanut oil*

8 ounces bean sprouts

2 scallions, chopped

1 garlic clove, crushed

2 tablespoons soy sauce

2 teaspoons sesame oil

1 tablespoon sesame seeds

2 tablespoons chopped fresh cilantro

salt and ground black pepper

COOK'S TIP

*You can buy beans for
sprouting at most health food
stores. Follow the directions on
the package to produce your
own sprouts for this stir-fry.
Bean sprouts can be stored in
the fridge for up to two days.*

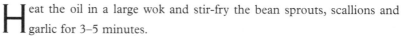eat the oil in a large wok and stir-fry the bean sprouts, scallions and garlic for 3–5 minutes.

Add the soy sauce, sesame oil, sesame seeds and chopped cilantro, with plenty of salt and pepper to taste. Toss over the heat for 1–2 more minutes and serve.

AVOCADO AND CILANTRO SALAD DIP

A bowl of this creamy cilantro dip is wonderful with crudités, tortilla chips and crispy potato skins.

Serves 4

2 large ripe avocados

2 garlic cloves, crushed

1 small onion, finely chopped

¼ cup lemon juice

1 fresh green chili, seeded and
  chopped (optional)

3 tablespoons chopped fresh cilantro

salt

Tabasco sauce, to taste

To serve

5 large potatoes

1 tablespoon vegetable oil

4 celery sticks, cut into fingers

3 large ripe tomatoes, cut into wedges

1 mild Spanish onion, cut into strips

tortilla chips

Cut the avocados in half, lengthwise, discard the pits and scoop the flesh into a food processor or blender. Add the garlic, onion, lemon juice and chopped green chili, if using. Process roughly. Add the cilantro, and season to taste with salt and Tabasco sauce. Cover tightly with plastic wrap to prevent discoloration.

Prepare the potato skins. Peel the potatoes thickly, aiming for 6–8 large pieces of peel from each one. Place the skins in a saucepan, pour in boiling water to cover and cook for 5 minutes. Preheat the broiler. Drain the potato skins well, toss them in oil, season with salt and broil them until crisp.

Transfer the avocado dip to an attractive bowl. Serve with the potato skins, crudités and tortilla chips.

CURRIED CILANTRO AND PARSNIP PIE

Sweet, creamy parsnips are beautifully complemented by the addition of cilantro and cheese. This unusual but delicious combination of flavors makes for a very tasty pie.

Serves 4

1 cup flour

½ cup butter

1 egg yolk, beaten with
   2 teaspoons water

salt and ground black pepper

For the filling

8 shallots, peeled

2 large parsnips, thinly sliced

2 carrots, thinly sliced

2 tablespoons butter or margarine

2 tablespoons whole wheat flour

1 tablespoon mild curry or
   tikka paste

1¼ cups milk

1 cup grated aged cheese

3 tablespoons chopped fresh cilantro

Put the flour in a mixing bowl. Add plenty of salt and pepper, then rub in the butter until the mixture resembles bread crumbs. Add just enough water to bind the dough, then wrap it in plastic wrap and set it aside in a cool place while you make the filling.

Put the shallots, parsnips and carrots in a saucepan with just enough water to cover. Bring to a boil and blanch the vegetables for 5 minutes. Drain, reserving about 1¼ cups of the liquid.

Melt the butter in a clean pan. Stir in the flour and curry paste. Cook for 1 minute, then gradually whisk in the reserved stock and milk until smooth. Bring to a boil, stirring constantly, then lower the heat and simmer for 1–2 minutes. Take the pan off the heat, stir in the cheese and seasoning, then mix into the vegetables with the cilantro. Pour into a pie dish, and place a pie funnel in the center. Let cool.

Preheat the oven to 400°F. Roll out the pastry to a round large enough to fit the top of the pie dish. Re-roll the trimmings into long strips. Brush the pastry edges with egg yolk wash and fit the pastry strips on the edge of the dish. Brush again with egg yolk wash, then fit the lid over the funnel. Cut off the overhanging pastry and crimp the edges. Cut a hole for the funnel, brush with the remaining egg yolk wash and make decorations with the trimmings, glazing them too. Bake for 25–30 minutes, until the pie crust is golden brown and crisp. Serve immediately.

CHARGRILLED VEGETABLES WITH CILANTRO SALSA

Enjoy a delightful meal with these chunky chargrilled vegetables served hot with a no-cook cilantro salsa.

Serves 4

1 large sweet potato, cut in
   thick slices
2 zucchini, halved lengthwise
2 red bell peppers, quartered
olive oil, for brushing

For the salsa

2 large tomatoes, peeled and
   finely chopped
2 scallions, finely chopped
1 small green chili, chopped
juice of 1 small lime
2 tablespoons chopped fresh cilantro
salt and ground black pepper

Bring a small saucepan of lightly salted water to a boil. Add the sweet potato and parboil for 5 minutes, until it is barely tender. Drain and let cool.

Place the zucchini in a colander. Sprinkle with a little salt and let drain for 20 minutes, then rinse and pat dry.

Make the salsa by mixing all the ingredients together in a bowl. Cover and set aside for 30–45 minutes to allow the flavors to blend.

Meanwhile, light the grill. Put the sweet potato slices, zucchini and peppers on the grill rack or in a hinged basket and brush them with oil. Cook them until they are lightly charred and softened, brushing with oil again and turning at least once. Serve hot with the salsa.

TOMATO AND CILANTRO SALAD RELISH

There are many versions of this cilantro relish, which is the traditional accompaniment for an Indian curry. This one will leave your mouth feeling cool and fresh.

Serves 4

3 ripe tomatoes

2 scallions, chopped

¼ teaspoon superfine sugar

salt

3 tablespoons chopped fresh cilantro

Remove the tough cores from the tomatoes with a small knife. Cut them in half, remove the seeds and dice the flesh. Transfer the tomatoes to a bowl and add the scallions, sugar, salt and chopped cilantro. Mix well, cover and set aside for at least 30 minutes to allow the flavors to blend. Serve at room temperature.

COOK'S TIP
This salad relish also tastes wonderful with fresh crab, lobster or shellfish.

IMAM BAYILDI

This classic eggplant dish is accented with both ground coriander and fresh cilantro. According to legend, Imam Bayildi means "the Imam fainted," because he was so overcome by this delicious dish.

Serves 4

2 eggplants, halved lengthwise

¼ cup olive oil, plus extra
    if needed

2 large onions, thinly sliced

2 garlic cloves, crushed

1 green bell pepper, seeded and sliced

14-ounce can chopped tomatoes

3 tablespoons sugar

1 teaspoon ground coriander

2 tablespoons fresh chopped cilantro

salt and ground black pepper

crusty bread, to serve

cilantro sprigs, to serve

COOK'S TIP
Imam Bayildi can be served hot. It needs no accompaniment other than a bowl of plain yogurt and some crusty bread or nan.

Using a sharp knife, slash the flesh of the eggplants a few times. Place them in a colander, sprinkle the cut sides with salt and let sit for about 30 minutes. Rinse well and pat dry.

Preheat the oven to 375°F. Heat the oil in a frying pan, add the eggplants, cut-sides down, and fry for 5 minutes. Remove with a slotted spoon or tongs and place in a shallow ovenproof dish. Add the onions, garlic and green bell pepper to the pan, with extra oil if necessary, and cook for about 10 minutes, until the vegetables have softened. Add the tomatoes, sugar and ground coriander with salt and pepper to taste. Cook for about 5 minutes, until the mixture has reduced. Stir in the chopped cilantro.

Spoon this mixture on top of the eggplants. Cover and bake for 30–35 minutes. Cool, then chill. Serve cold with crusty bread, garnished with cilantro sprigs.

INDEX

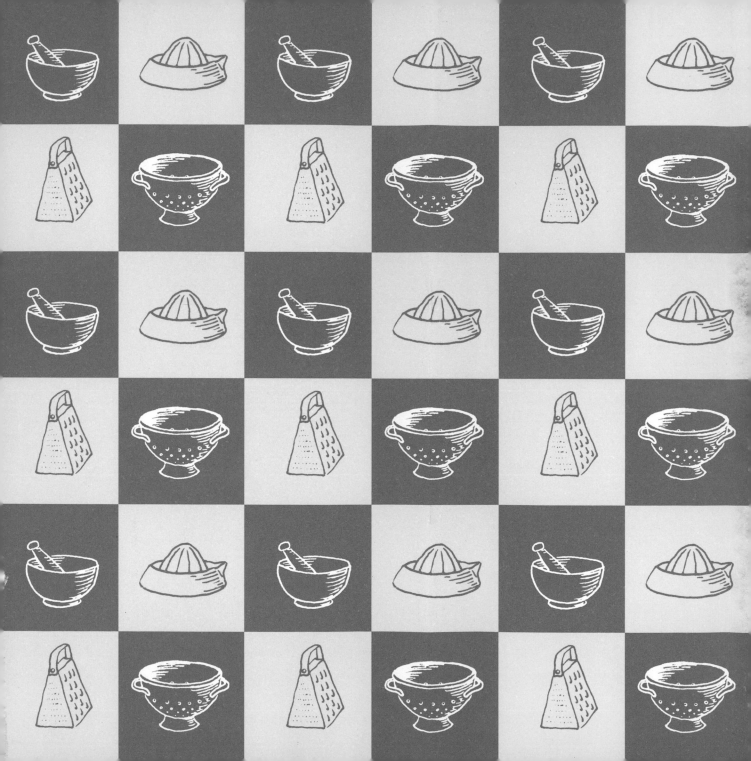